SUCCESS BEGINS FROM WHERE YOU ARE!

Michael Forde

Disclaimer

Copyright © 2017

All Rights Reserved – Michael Forde

ALL RIGHTS RESERVED.
No part of this publication may be reproduced or transmitted in any form whatsoever, electronic, or mechanical, including photocopying, recording, or by any informational storage or retrieval system without written, dated and signed permission from the author.

Dalia,

Thank you for being such a great coworker! Wishing you the best in all that you do!

Your friend,
Michael Forde

Dedication

This book is dedicated to all those who aspire to become successful in life, but find a veiled force impeding their start. It is for all those who find it difficult to decipher the route to success, and need help, guidance, courage, and belief to begin the journey.

Table of Contents

Introduction — 9

CHAPTER 1: DEFINING SUCCESS — 12

CHAPTER 2: IMPORTANCE OF MENTORS — 17

   Mentorship — 17

   The Significance — 17

CHAPTER 3: LOSING THE STRINGS — 22

   External Strings — 23

     Peer Pressure — 24

     The Company — 25

   Internal Strings — 27

     Procrastination — 27

     Experience vs. Regret — 29

     The Hoax of Complacency — 30

CHAPTER 4: BABY STEPS TO SUCCESS — 32

   Step #1: Dream the Dream — 33

   Step #2: Draw a Time Frame — 33

   Step #3: Organization — 34

CHAPTER 5: MINDSET AND PRACTICES — 36

Never Back Down	37
No Blame Games	38
Smart Risks	39
CHAPTER 6: TURNING THE TABLES	**41**
Courage and Commitment	42
Self Dependence	42
Drive and Passion	43
Denial	43
Reality Vs Fantasy	44
In a Nutshell	44
CHAPTER 7: BRINGING IT ALL TOGETHER	**46**
Conclusion	**48**

Introduction

If only you were given a dollar for every other productive idea that you had, you would have already been a millionaire! Unfortunately, things are not as effortless as they seem. The reality is cruel, and those who only daydream seldom reach the peaks of Mountain Glory.

Creativity is often thought to exist among a handful of people on earth. This is a false notion, and undoubtedly a primal reason of lowered self-esteem among the majority. The aspect of ingenuity, the art of producing something from nothing—the absolute skill of creativity—resides in every human being.

Then what exactly is it that made Warren Buffet 'Warren Buffet' and Steve Jobs 'Steve Jobs'? If every man and woman on earth has a spark of creativeness hidden inside of them, then what is it that differentiates them from the elite masterminds of the world?

This difference—this analogy between the top-notch minds—will be explored in this book where I will discuss their roads to success. *'Success Begins From Where You Are!'* is a book that will prove that all you need is a push to reach the top. It will help you get a kick-start towards the summit you are destined for!

Have you ever thought about what made a businessman like Ralph Lauren reach the height of success that he enjoys ever so contentedly? Or what led Steve Jobs to writing a page in the books of history? It is their perseverance!

You might have heard that being headstrong pays off in life. No doubt it does! It did for Howard Shultz and Chris Gardner. But the question is not about whether being willful assists in achieving success or not.

The question is this—how exactly do you ignite that willfulness that sparks within yourself to get up and get moving, that stubbornness to keep going even if battered? This is what the real question should be, and this is what the right question is! This book will answer this question and many more of the sort.

Want to know something great and uplifting in the meantime? You are already on the right track. You are already on the road to success. All you need to do is pace up! Surprised much? Well, you might not know this, but in life there is only one road to take. For some, that road may be a bit smoother; for others, it is not.

Always remember that failure is not the end. Think of it as a point on the road to success. No matter how many of those points you cross, you will, at some point, reach the stop that says, 'success'. All you need to do is to keep moving.

Now, there may be some short-term successes or multiple failures, but always bear in mind that these are just a few pit stops along the way. Bear in mind that these are just hurdles or negligible rewards—in case you've been hitting 'success points' more often.

Once you cross those hurdles, once you beat the failures, once your break the enchantment, you will be welcomed by that bright light—that summit of success where you'll be handed over the trophy of your triumph.

Do remember what Will Smith says in the movie, 'The Pursuit of Happyness',

> *"Don't ever let somebody tell you that you can't do something."*

That is because you sure can!

All you need is a little help, a little kick-start. A little motivation!

CHAPTER 1: DEFINING SUCCESS

"Success means having the courage, the determination, and the will to become the person you believe you were meant to be."

– George Sheehan

Success is a fairly broad term. Every person perceives it in a different manner, which tends to make this a vague term. This is apparently where the problem begins. When we go out and set our goals in life, we base it on the term 'success', yet we have no clue what the word means. We have no clue what success actually is.

Some define success as monetary kingship—most people to be honest—while others attribute it to a certain commodity. Say, for instance, one person might believe he is successful if he becomes a millionaire. No matter what he or she does or achieves prior to becoming a millionaire, the outlook on life is deemed as a pit-stop.

On the other hand, there is this other person who has attributed success to, let's say, owning a house. The person might not be a millionaire, but if he pays off the mortgage on time, it is a tag of success for him!

This is where you start off on the wrong foot. You go on to define success based on someone else's definition of the term, and base your goals on that—not the best way to go about it.

So if the term has a different meaning for everyone, does that mean that it does not have an underlining definition to itself? Is there nothing that generalizes what the actuality of this term is? Well, as it stands, there is: there is something that lays the basis for success. That subject to most people's neglect is belief!

Mahatma Gandhi once said,

> "If I have the belief that I can do it, I shall surely acquire the capacity to do it"

Believe it or not, 'belief' is the one thing that stands between you and your definition of success. It is the only thing that defines the correlation between the successful people, despite the angle you choose to view it from. It is the foremost thing to acquire while routing for your journey uphill.

Belief and hope coincide with each other. When you believe that you can do something, it gives rise to hope—a factor that provokes your will to 'get up and get moving'. It is this underlying definition of success that helps you pass the mist that curtains your success from you.

This brings us back to square one. What is success? We know that belief is something that drives you to success, but how do you know what success is for you in the first place? What do you have that belief for? Where are you headed with it?

This is of great significance. Part of the reason for this is that you have to set the right basis for your way down the road. On the bright side, it is not something that would require an intervention. It is what comes from within. A light buried within your unconscious mind that knows what you intend to become, an innate feeling that defines success for you. All you need to do is find that light—your desire to work for it will come as a consequence.

But then again, how do you find that bright light within which defines what success is for you? Seems complicated, right? Well, it isn't. All you ought to do is find what you love. You have to find that place where your passion lies. Once you find that, it will lead you to your very own definition of success.

Henry Hazlitt defines the matter impeccably,

> *"A strong passion for any object will ensure success, for the desire of the end will point out the means."*

That 'object', however, does not necessarily need to be a commodity. As I mentioned, it can be anything that ignites the spark. It is a chain process of simple, but interconnected short steps that go on to paint the big picture for you.

Everything boils down to the core of it—what you love to do. Once you grab hold of your passion, something you avidly put your efforts into, things go uphill from there. For starters, it will help you define the right goal for you, the definition of success in your life.

As Henry said, once you have found that feeling of affection for something, it will pull the tools you need to triumph towards you. For Chris Gardner, it was the love for a Ferrari 308 convertible. He considered it necessary to know what he needed to conquer in order to own such a convertible, and so he did. The rest of the puzzle came together by his belief. He knew he could do what he needed to do despite being a man without a home.

So how do I define success? For me, it is something that puts you in pursuit of something greater. Understand success as an unending aspect of life. As long as you are moving uphill, you are successful. That is what success is for me.

When you are defining success, whatever it is for you, first lay down the basis of belief. Trust yourself! Believe yourself! Think of all the people who started from where you stand right now. Even better, think of the people who began their journey from a point far behind you. They made it because they believed! You can too!

While you start believing in yourself, do remember that there are those who will bring you down. There are those who will tell you that you cannot. But that is where resilience comes in.

> *"Don't ever let somebody tell you that you can't do something."*

The very same people who kick you when you are down will worship your triumphant version. So back to the original question, 'What is the definition of success?' Apparently, there is no right answer, but there is a right process. Start off by believing that you can do anything and have the power to do so. Find something that you really want, and start working for it with the utmost zeal.

By the time you acquire it, you will already have a better, much higher aim for yourself. Never give up hope. Never give up that belief within yourself. There will come a time when you will stand tall and successful! That will be the day when you will look back in astonishment, wondering how you achieved so much, just by believing. That will be the day when you will look upon the next summit to conquer! And *nothing* will stop you.

CHAPTER 2: IMPORTANCE OF MENTORS

"Mentor: someone whose hindsight can become your foresight."

– Anonymous

I cannot emphasize enough on the importance of a mentor. This becomes even truer when 'Success' is the subject matter. To comprehend it better, let us discuss the concept of mentorship.

Mentorship

By definition, it is the guidance provided by a person who has experience in what you ought to achieve or learn.

I refer to mentorship as the opportunity to make mistakes without making them. Perplexing, right? Well, not really. The concept of mentorship is all about confronting lesser obstacles. It is about knowing solutions before encountering potential problems. Mentorship is your insight to what could be, and the way to go about it.

The Significance

You can either be stagnant in life or be mobile. There is no third state. As long as you are not in the former one, you are doing alright. Not great, but alright. To be successful, however, you have to do better.

"Have to do better!" Tough words these are. This small bundle of words is enough to give rise to a mountain of confounding questions in your mind. Who is supposed to answer them? I am sure someone will, right?

Yes, someone will! That 'someone' is the mentors. They are your solution to the huge pile of questions, your key to take the next step forward. Without a mentor, your way ahead will be hazy. You will be moving forward, in the right direction even, but the hurdles that lie there will only appear when you come too close to them. You will not have the time to react. Although you won't relinquish your pursuit of greatness, it will surely cost you time, and I need not explain that 'time is money.'

Here, the haze is your level of uncertainty moving forward, and the hurdles, well, hurdles! This is where the mentors come in. They have been there and done that. They know what you can expect at each point of your journey. The fact that they are who they are today is a living proof that they know just the ways to solve a potential problem.

Better yet, mentors are also the people who can help greatly in kicking it off, since most of the people who have achieved great levels of success started from the very bottom.

I referred to mentorship as making mistakes without making them. This is mostly because your mentors are the ones who have made mistakes for you to learn from. They allow you to go by your chosen lane, and yet not encounter the problems they did. You can smoothen your road to a great extent by forming sophisticated ways out—that too, in advance!

However, an unfortunate notion prevails among us that bars us from making the most of the mentorship—looking up to a single person for guidance. You need to understand that when you oversee the importance of mentorship, you tend to lose a great deal of vision. You hold yourself back from a vast range of experiences that can play a factor in your impending success.

Every mentor sheds light upon a different angle to the same story. They all became successful, but none of them went through the exact same path. Every person brings along some unique aspect of knowledge—one that lets it stand out from the rest. Even you will face some unforeseen and unanticipated intricacies that will give you your inimitable identity. This is inevitable!

Mentorship is about lowering the absolute: lessening the most obvious hurdles along the way. So when you finally encounter that unique bewilderment, you have the energy and the confidence to take it on like a pro!

The learning from practical experiences and lessening of the obstacles is just an aspect of the importance of mentorship. I cannot emphasize it enough!

"So having a mentor is important. But how do I know I have the right mentor?" If a person is successful by your definition of success, you can make him or her your mentor. There is no rigidity in who can be your mentor and who cannot.

It can be your parents, your closest friends, a celebrity, anyone! Anyone who has the characteristics you wish you had. Anyone who has the characteristics that make them who they are! By that, it does not mean that you must have only one mentor. You may even have a couple! In fact, having more than a single mentor tends to be a far better practice while in pursuit of success.

There is always that one person that stands out among the rest for you. This is the main person that you can look up to for leadership. You can have a couple of other mentors as well.

According to Saygil Yalcin—Owner of SellAnyCar, and a billionaire entrepreneur—picking the distinctiveness of several mentors is the key to success.

In other words, Saygil believes that apart from your central mentor, you should acquire the best traits of every mentor of yours. Learn from the experiences of many. This blend of character and experience will put forward a more firm character. Add your distinctive skill and experience, and you will welcome an image that is superior to any one of the mentors individually—that superior image is yours!

So it doesn't matter how you go about it, the importance of mentors always remain undisputed. They are your guide to success! Read them well, take as much help you can get from them, learn from their mistakes, learn how they crafted their own path to success, and follow their footsteps in your own unique way.

One more thing that you should bear in mind about having a mentor is that it is not just about their work and how they managed to jump over their hurdles. It is also about inspiration.

If you have a mentor that inspires you, chances are that you will do great things in life! You will achieve the levels of success you never thought you would. You will reach the heights of glory you never thought were even in your grasp. Most of all, you will stay motivated in your endeavor to achieve success. This is the power of mentorship.

Does that sound shallow to you? Well, these have been fact checked and proven to be correct! MENTOR—The National Mentoring Partnership—revealed that young students who were not doing well in different aspects of life are 130% more likely to secure a leadership role once they have a mentor to look up to.

That is the power of mentorship. You don't see it upfront, but once the bigger picture unveils itself, you begin to realize the astounding impact it made. As I mentioned earlier, I simply cannot emphasize enough on the importance of a mentor.

The best part is, you can fit in your mentor's shoes pretty well. Want to know why? Well, because they once stood right where you stand in life right now. This is exactly where they took off from. They too, were once misguided. They too, once roamed around, searching for answers.

Don't lose hope. Keep that self-belief, and have a mentor who can build up and fuel that spark within you. Have a mentor so you know what you need to do to reach where you are headed! Before you know it, you will be standing tall on the summit of success; before you know it, you yourself would have become a mentor to someone else. This is how the chain works! Be a part of it, and unravel the preeminent path to success!

CHAPTER 3: LOSING THE STRINGS

"If you're absent during my struggle, don't expect to be present during my success."

– Will Smith

The road to success may pose challenges, but it does not stop you from moving forward. What does stop you, however, are the strings.

The biggest stumbling block in the road to success is getting on it in the first place. In other words, the most difficult aspect of summiting greatness is not about conquering the road; it is about losing the strings that hold you back—the strings that keep you stagnant!

When you are stagnant, or moving with a slow pace in life, you are unaware of your unnecessary ties. You fail to comprehend how these strings that are attached to you can cause a dent in your pursuit to greatness. Think of it as numerous large ropes attached to your waist. These ropes are loose and don't stop you from moving, unless you pass a point where they stretch to the max.

Unfortunately, the strings that we have attached to ourselves are all too short. In other words, the moment you take a leap forward, you will be pulled back by one thing or the other. It is merely a frivolity! This is not even the worst part.

The most terrible aspect of having unnecessary strings attached is that not only do they pull you back, but they also tend to lessen your desire to move forward. This is no different than a crab going round and round in a bucket. Those that fall behind, those who lack belief, those unlike you, ensure stagnancy around them.

Now that you understand the adversity of the superfluous strings attached, it is time to let you in on what these attachments are in reality. It is always much of a shocker. Things which may seem close to you, or people you may think of as your alliance, pledge no allegiance!

The 'strings' in real life can be separated into two parts: the externals and the internals. In the case of the former, you are held back by something or someone other than yourself, while the latter finds you, yourself, as the culprit. It is concerned with your traits that cast the negative spell on you!

Before we move forward, I would like to show you the bright side of it. No matter who or what drags you down, what I am referring to as 'strings' are sheer futile filaments. You can break them down and cut them off with the slightest of your efforts, marking your first step towards success.

The following section will shed light upon the external strings in life that you need to get rid of before you set off on your journey.

External Strings

Although there are not as many external pulls as those which are internal, the ones you are hooked to cast an immense shadow of darkness over the road ahead.

Peer Pressure

The last thing that you would want in your life is to fall under peer pressure. This is one of the primary reasons why so many people fail to get a kick-start or a boost.

The aspect of peer pressure that makes it hugely detrimental is that you don't come to realize that you are being pulled back. It might seem to you as just another thing someone is telling you to do or not to do. What you lack is the bigger picture.

It is most often than not that people fail to see the long-term consequence of negative peer pressure. There have, in fact, been several studies on the topic. Pressure from the peers to do or to not do something always manages to top the lists.

A negative pull by a peer can be in any manner. You may have just started believing in your abilities to do something. You may have just started to reconcile your scattered thoughts and gotten the courage to take a step forward. Whilst you do so, a peer may bring down your drive, tamper your belief, and make you believe that what you are setting out to achieve is impossible.

Nothing is impossible, provided that you prime your mind and work for it with zest and zeal.

You see, the mind of a person is a very beautiful and powerful thing. No matter who you are or what you do, it has the ability to believe if you tell it something. It is a matter of what you feed your brain with. If you continue to put negative thoughts in it, your brain will hinder your progress. It will, at one point, start

believing that you won't be able to achieve much—
this is where the recession begins.

Propitiously, you can alter that, but my question is,
why go there in the first place? Why not make the
point you are at right now, the beginning point in
your journey?

The bottom line is this - people will bring you down.
People will pull your leg. That is because either they
themselves lack self-esteem, or they just envy your
potential to succeed. Whichever the reason may be,
unconstructive pressure from a peer is not something
that will assist you in moving uphill. Giving up might
seem like the easier thing to do, but easier does not
always mean better.

The road to success is bumpy, and success only
comes to those who strive for it. It only comes to
those that come out of their bubble, who decide to
conquer the bumpy road that comes in their way.

The Company

This part is somewhat related to 'Peer Pressure', but
is not quite the same. You must have heard the
phrase, 'A man is known by the company he keeps'
pretty often! It cannot get truer than this. The reason
is quite simple. Humans are designed in a way which
reflects continuous learning. It is an essential aspect
of life. No matter what you do or how old you are, you
always keep learning from your surroundings.

So if you keep a company that pulls you away from
taking a step forward, from routing towards
greatness, from thinking big, then there may come a
time when your mind will adapt to the negativity. It

will start to believe that taking a step forward might not be the wiser alternative.

Sounds so cliché, right? Sadly a cliché is a cliché for a reason. It happens! This is why keeping a positive company is injected into your mind from the day you are born.

Jim Rohn—An American Entrepreneur—said,

> *"You are the average of the five people you spend the most time with."*

In other words, you are likely to become a pessimist if those around you are pessimists, and vice versa.

"So do I leave my company entirely?"

Not really. However, you do need to keep away from it for the most part of the day. Surround yourself with those who see the glass as being half full. Build a social circle that compels you to take the next step. Join the group that pulls out the best in you!

The extent to which this diminutive attempt to get up and get moving will help you is just unbelievable. Don't let that hope die within you. Do not let your success be a figment of your imagination. You believe in yourself now. It is time to surround yourself with a company that assists your constructive thought process.

Do bear one thing in mind: 'No company' is better than 'Bad company'! If anything, you will divest the attire of external strings that pull you back.

Internal Strings

I said that having no company is better than having a bad circle of peers. So does that mean that you are in safe hands? No, you are not! There is one more enemy to defeat to have a kick-start. That adversary is your internal strings—your traits that cuff your feet to the ground.

Procrastination

If there is anything that you need to purge from within yourself, it is procrastination!

Procrastination: Sounds like such a plain word, right? The effects of it say differently.

Did you know that four out of ten people go on to face monetary loss only as a consequence of procrastination? GURA annual report – 2008 mentioned this statistic after comprehensive research. The number is considered to have risen with time.

The worst part about this evil is that it keeps you in the midst of an infinite road, a road that takes you to no man's land. It does not let you take the initial step, the kick-start. This is, in actuality, the only spell that it casts over you—a spell that lays the basis of unproductiveness. Procrastination does not let you proceed.

On the brighter side, procrastination is not as difficult to fight. I knew I was wasting time doing nothing, but there was something that held me from getting up, and being on the move—a force to be reckoned with.

It took me a little time to figure this out, but you will not believe how simple the key to getting rid of procrastination was! You see, the problem is not that you defer the impending work. The issue lies somewhere else. It lies in over-thinking stuff. That, right there, is the root cause of procrastination.

Give it a thought. Why do you put off something you are meant to commit yourself to? Let me rephrase that for you – why do you put off something you are meant to do?

In procrastination, we only tend to blame our laziness. In reality, there is a lot that causes us to become lethargic in the first place. For me, the driving factor of procrastination was over-thinking.

Whenever I thought of doing something I was supposed to, I would mirror the entire process in my mind, thinking of all the steps I had to go through to get the job done. Simultaneously, the drowning thoughts led me to something else that I could invest my time and effort in, often an act of leisure.

So there I was, thinking about how I over-think stuff. I barred myself from committing my mind to pointless thoughts. When I had to do something, I went for it. This slowly began the eradication of procrastination.

The point here is that procrastination is always driven by something. It could be the fear of failing in a crucial step on the way that causes you to procrastinate, or it could be an alternate act of leisure that becomes the driver.

Of course, there is always a risk that you don't plan out things perfectly, but, as Mark Zuckerberg says,

"The biggest risk is not taking any risk."

So the next time you find yourself lying back on your couch, excusing yourself from a job that needs to be done, take a moment, stop thinking, and *just do it*. You will be astonished to see how one thing leads to another once you get on your feet and start moving.

Experience vs. Regret

Everyone regrets making mistakes, but wise men don't. It is a perspective of thought. Regretting is fine—if accompanied with the next endeavor—rebuttal is not! You need to accept the reality of things and move on.

Remember what Thomas A. Edison said?

"I have not failed. I've just found 10,000 ways that won't work."

Every other successful figure that you can think of failed, and not just once; they failed numerous times. But that did not bring them down. The rock bottom they hit was cushioned by their zeal to succeed, their belief to rise back up again. This is what differentiates those who win from those who don't.

Did you ever think about any good that could come from only sitting back and regretting the failure in the initial attempts to reach the peak of Mountain Glory? Apparently, there is none, unless you let it go. Each mistake and each failure is, as Edison said, a method that you are to refrain from in the future.

Keep your hopes up! Keep believing in yourself! Learn, don't regret! That drive to succeed will let you bear in mind the summit you are destined for. It will allow you to get things on the go. It will let you cut the strings loose so you can begin your journey uphill.

The Hoax of Complacency

It is good to be complacent with what you have, but this does not mean that you should kill that craving for success. Being successful, as mentioned earlier, is not something definitive. Once you have flagged your success on that peak you routed for, rest for a while, and route for a spot much higher than that.

But what happens when you have not kicked off yet? What happens if you think that you are content with where you stand at the moment?

To state it in the simplest of the terms, you lose reason in life. Complacency in being stagnant is not the choice of the wise.

Often times than not, this is a subconscious excuse to not work for it. It is a subliminal belief that you will not be able to achieve something that you want to, and your mind tricks you into thinking you don't want it at all. This is why it is a hoax. This is why it is a string that does not allow you to move forward in life. That is why this is a string you desperately need to get rid of.

To get your mind on the right track and to get over this hoax of complacency, find something that entices you. Look for something that you want and don't have. Life becomes meaningless when you don't have something to look forward to. Once you have found something that you are willing to work for, this is when you cut off the internal string attached. And don't forget: *Nothing* is impossible.

When you come to think about it, it is not the external strings that pull you back as much as the internal strings. It is your negative traits that often bar you from getting that kick-start. In other words, you have to work more on the traits that bar you from beginning your journey, and then cut off ties with the external ones.

Remember, the more you lessen the negative strings attached, the easier your transition will be from rigidity to being mobile towards success. The lesser strings there are, the more flexible you will become.

CHAPTER 4: BABY STEPS TO SUCCESS

"Take one step at a time but reflect on where each step is taking you."

– Mary-Frances Winters

Success is subjective. We have talked about that in the beginning of this book. But is there anything that can streamline it? Is there anything that helps you predefine the path to take?

Is there something that I can partition my road to success into?

This is a question that holds utmost importance while you route for success. It lets you analyze what you are headed for. You get to mark the spot that you are to reach and where you stand at the moment in the inevitable journey.

The reason why I deem this question as being of immense significance is that it plays a key role in your ride from one end to the other. It is what drives hope in you. This is what strengthens your belief to succeed.

Let me unveil in front of you, the 'baby steps to success'.

To comprehend them better, think of them as a token of appreciation for what you have achieved so far. As you keep moving uphill, as you keep passing each step, it injects a sense of self-belief, a sense of fulfillment in you. It is these steps to success that streamline what you ought to achieve, and how you are to do it.

These steps are also correlated which means you cannot hop on to the next unless you have cleared the one you stand at, at the moment.

Step #1: Dream the Dream

The biggest hurdle, the prevailing issue in setting out to acquire success, is that people don't dream their dream. This does not mean that you are shying away from owning that sports car, or have given up on being a renowned healthcare professional. It just means that whatever your definition of success is, you are not wholehearted about it.

This is no different than a slippery terrain. Your efforts are unlikely to bring you near the goal. You need to first firmly place your feet on the ground. When I say 'Dream the Dream', what I point towards is the will to fulfill it. Unless you believe that you are meant to turn that dream into reality, unless you dream to fulfill your dream, you will not be able to conquer what the road throws at you.

My advice is, don't just dream of accomplishing it. This often creates doubts—a mountain of "Whys" in your head. Dream the dream! Think of the times you will have achieved it. Imagine your life with the dream fulfilled. Imagine yourself successful.

In addition to all the efforts put in, just the thought of having won what you ought to achieve augments the probability of a win—this adds to your chances of ending up successful!

Step #2: Draw a Time Frame

Letting yourself loose is not the best thing to do, especially if you are in the pursuit of success. You need to organize your efforts in a certain frame of time. Let me explain why.

When you walk free, when you don't have a deadline to meet, you are more likely to lose track. The chances that you will stray from your goal to achieve success increases exponentially! You are not at fault here. We all do this. This is basic human nature. We procrastinate when we have a decent time frame. I don't think I need to force much attention to the adversities of procrastination anymore!

Time frames are proven to bring out the best in you. They sharpen your skills and polish your expertise that plays a factor in summiting the mountain. They bind you, and force the abilities out that you never thought you had.

Set a deadline. Plan out by when exactly you strive to achieve your goal. This will poke at the laziness and provoke action from within you!

Step #3: Organization

Once you have defined your goal, acquire the belief to accomplish it, and set a deadline to meet that goal. It is time to organize the path. It is time to plan segments of the road you are about to take. These segments will help keep you on the route and follow the time frame.

This is another important step towards success. You see, when you lack organization, although you are mobile, your plans are haphazard! This jumble consequently ruins the deadline you are determined to meet, taking down the entire structure to become triumphant.

Of course, you don't stop there. Your zest and zeal picks you up and leads you to your divine point, but the road that is already under construction becomes even more damaged. Why would you want to make things difficult? No one would. It is all about playing it smart. Smoothen the route as much as you possibly can—organize it.

Plan what steps you need to take to get to the top, distribute them along the road, and follow them! It will not take long for you to conquer the mountain you have set yourself out for with this approach.

The time you spend organizing your path never goes in vain, ever! In the words of Benjamin Franklin,

"For every minute spent organizing, an hour is earned!"

CHAPTER 5: MINDSET AND PRACTICES

"Whatever the mind of man can conceive and believe, it can achieve"

– Napoleon Hill

You must have heard the ever so famous line, *"Leaders are born, not made."* Well, I disagree! There are not many traits that an infant brings along into this world, and fortunately, those that he or she does, are shared by every last human being on earth.

There are three major innate characteristics of a human being: the reflexes, the curiosity, and the impulse to fool around. Certain psychologists also believe that some individuals might find it easier to interpret expressions during infancy—a slight head-start, don't you think? However, there is not much that defines which newborn will go on to be successful and which one won't.

If you ponder a little, I mentioned in the very first chapter of the book that the definition of success varies between individuals. And that definition is only explored when you grow up a little, when you explore and find that piece of luring extravaganza which attracts all your focus.

My point is, how can something innate define the goal—the success you are bound to accomplish—when that goal or that definition does not even exist when you are born?

One of my friends and I had a discussion pertaining to the subject once. I won't lay down the entire discussion, but we both agreed at one thing right at the end - sure, some genetic may abilities assist you in becoming successful, but *"Leaders are born, not made"* is still a false notion. Anything that others can do to become successful, you can too! It is all about the eagerness, the desire that burns within you to reach the summit of success.

In the words of Suzie Wokabi,

> *"It is not easy to break into or be successful... Success stories all revolve around extreme passion."*

But there is something that distinguishes those who plant their flag on the pinnacle from those who struggle. The good thing is that each and every single trait that parts the two can be mastered by you! Sounds relieving, right? That's because it is!

Let us jump into the traits that assist one in reaching the top—the traits that you can acquire just with a little effort.

Never Back Down

One thing, a pretty big of a thing that draws the line between you and the popular figures, is aspiration - the belief that no matter what happens, there is always light at the end of the tunnel.

I have mentioned this in the past, I am stating it now, and I will continue to talk about it in the coming chapters of this book:

> *'Failure is just a point on the road to success'.*

As you cross a point, you get more mature, more experienced, and the best of all—closer to your goal!

It is very unfortunate that the word 'failure' has been attributed to unsuccessfulness today! If you come to think of it, it is these failures that make you successful in life. It is these failures that make your success story worth listening to.

If a failure lets you down, I have a great tip for you! Write it down somewhere. When you finally reach the point you are destined for, you would have a bunch of stories to tell your mentees! You might even get a Hollywood hit out of it. (Remember Pursuit of Happyness?)

Always remember: all successful people go through failures. Learn to embrace it. The good part is, if you are meeting such pit stops, you are already on your way to greatness! Just don't let anything go. Keep striving—all successful people do!

These words by Zig Ziglar—a famous American author—are one of my all-time favorites,

> "Yesterday ended last night."

No Blame Games

Let me get one thing straight. No one is accustomed to helping you in your endeavors. The borderline difference between the greats and the struggling is that the former don't waste time playing the blame game. If something goes wrong, they ponder into the moves that did not work, and redo with a little restrictedness.

If something or someone is letting you down, find a way around it! Look into things a little differently. Propel your ability to ponder! The good news is that there are dozens of different angles that can be used. You just have to find the one that works.

Smart Risks

The ability to take risks is a major characteristic of successful people. What bothers me is that everyone tells youngsters to take risks as this is an important aspect of success. But no one guides them on the level they need to maintain.

Risks define the element of success. Every person who has ever reached to the top jumped into the unforeseen. However, this does not mean that you should dive in nose down! While taking risks is indispensable, measuring it as a prerequisite is also of great significance.

This means that there will be times in your journey when you would have to lunge without being able to depict the potential outcome. It can either upset your voyage for a little while or pass by, giving you a dose of confidence and a supplement of experience. Either way, what you need to ensure is that the risks you take are calculated. You don't want to lose it all in the gamble. Always take steps with a backup plan, and avoid putting all of your eggs in one basket.

A great way to take the leap is to study stories that relate well to what you route for: someone who has been through such an anomaly and has carved a way around it. If anything, this injects in you a bunch of possibilities to lessen the risk and the cost you may bear.

It cannot be better than what Walter Wriston said,

> *"Life is more risk management, rather than exclusion of risks"*

This beautiful set of words explains that risk is not something that you can or should avoid. It is something that you should plan out for in order to cut off as much of the danger tied to it as possible.

CHAPTER 6: TURNING THE TABLES

"When everything seems to be going against you, remember that the airplane takes off against the wind, not with it."

– Henry Ford

By this point, you will have comprehended the fact that success is not something that is predefined by genetics. Nor is it something unachievable. You just need the right key to unlock the doors and to conquer the road.

However, there are some characteristics that are found commonly in successful people. They live life in a certain way, follow a mutual set of principles that most others don't. What boggles my mind is that those set of principles, those traits of success, are some of the simplest in life. In all honesty, I have yet to see an attribute of the elite that a layperson cannot get their hands on.

If that's the case, then why isn't everyone successful? Why isn't everyone as rich as Warren Buffet and as successful as Bill Gates? It is because not everyone follows the way of life followed by them. Some people, and I have seen this personally, think of that particular lifestyle as a cliché. And the modern mindset is all about avoiding the clichés.

I have jotted down the most effective characteristics commonly found in successful people. These characteristics will allow you to turn the tables in your life. They will let you embrace success that has been waiting to welcome you with open arms.

Courage and Commitment

If you want to have the caliber of a successful person, you need to show some courage. You need to prove that you are committed to what you have set out for. Name your icon and I can assure you that he or she has proven their drive and commitment to become an elite.

The standards of courage successful people enjoy are quite enormous. This is what differentiates them from others. You should have that drive too. And it only comes when you are committed to having something. It only drives you when you are passionate about reaching your goals.

You must be willing to do what the majority has stepped back from. You should be eager to run that extra mile others don't. Find a goal and stick to it. Stay committed and don't be afraid to take a step others are reluctant to.

Bear in mind that successful people are not common people. You need to take a different route. Do things in your own unique way. You are destined for sheer greatness, and that is what you should achieve—that is what you *can* achieve.

Self Dependence

"With great power comes great responsibility". You cannot run from responsibility. Those who have made it to the top, have the weight of the world on their shoulders. They just know how to manage it well!

"Thought" is an underrated word. Those who don't think of themselves as being successful from the very start, seldom make it to the top. This is the basis of this entire book. You need to believe in yourself. You need to take responsibility.

Only when you do that will you be able to learn how to handle it. It is the experiences that teach you how to bear the weight without losing control. This belief is what offers you the self-confidence, and the ability to take on things yourself.

Depending on yourself while making crucial decisions also adds to your ability to make decisions—something that comes in handy when you cross a certain point on the road uphill. In short, learn to make major decisions on your own. There are only a very limited number of times you can go wrong.

Drive and Passion

If you want to succeed in life, you need a driver. This driver is something that will keep you going. Most often than not, people confuse this part with independence, wherein actuality, it is a blend of a number of things. It is your will to succeed, your passion about whatever your dream is, and your stubbornness to reach the top, despite the hurdles life throws at you!

This blend is your driver. It is what lets you stay motivated and keep moving. This blend is what stands by you until you reach your destination, and even beyond that. It is what helps you conquer life as if it was a piece of cake!

Denial

Denial?

When we hear this word, we attribute it to negativity. Not the right way to look at it. You see, successful people are some of the biggest deniers you can think of. The way they deny what life throws at them is simply inexplicable.

Successful people deny failure!

And they deny it no matter how hard or how bad they fall. Call it their stubbornness, but they just do not accept failing. You must not accept falling behind and be complacent with anything less than sheer success! The best part is that you pretty easily can!

This saying summons it well,

> "Be stubborn about your goals and flexible about your methods."
>
> – Anonymous

Reality vs. Fantasy

Fantasizing about success is good; however, leaving it to be a figment of reality is not!

It is of utmost importance that you remain rational at all times through your journey. Want to hear something relieving? Being successful in life is a pretty rational thought—provided that you work for it. In other words, when you believe that you will be successful, and work your way for it, you will end up where you want to be!

In a Nutshell

There is no magic formula to anything. It is just the belief, the resilience, and the drive that allows you to reach the pinnacle of success. One thing that I strongly believe is to never give up. If you lose trust in your abilities to conquer your dream, the all-so-important traits needed to turn the tables will come falling down. Therefore, keep the pillar intact. Keep the dream alive with the drive! Let the traits of the elite assist you through your endeavors. You *will* find a way to your long-awaited success.

Walt Disney said,

> *"If you can dream it, you can do it"*

CHAPTER 7: BRINGING IT ALL TOGETHER

"The secret of getting ahead is getting started."

– Mark Twain

If you haven't yet, it is time to pack your things and leave for the inevitable journey. It is time to show fervor, and route for the pinnacle that awaits your arrival. It is time to bring it all together, and become successful!

By this point in the book, you know what success is all about, what aspects you need to consider, what traits you need to adapt to, and whose footsteps you need to follow. You just have to blend it all together!

The biggest hindrance in life is to think of success as something unachievable. Chris Gardner spent a night with his infant son in a public washroom. But his will, belief, and the unending desire to succeed made him the millionaire he is today. Steve Jobs worked from a garage to build Macintosh. He was kicked out of his own company, but refused to settle for that.

It is examples like these, and many more, that provide evidence of the sheer impact belief has. All you need is to back it up with action and who knows – you could be the author of the next page in history!

It is quite inspiring when you realize that you are no different from what every successful person once was. You are at no different place from where they once stood!

They devoted themselves, and did not want to settle for less, no matter what. It is complacency that deters your journey to the top of the mountain.

You want to know why I have emphasized 'belief' so much throughout the book? It is because it differentiates you from the rest of the people. A majority of people, unfortunately, tend to work hard to earn their bread and butter. But they don't envision themselves as people who can make it. They doubt their willfulness and their ability to become whatever they want to become. You might earn a buck that way, but the term 'success' might seem like a long shot to you.

Work hard, and find smarter ways to conquer hurdles. Learn from the experiences of others and add a touch of your own medicine to it. Set a revamped, more contemporary example for those to follow. Run with the mindset that hundreds of thousands of people are looking up to you and wish to follow your footsteps. Hundreds of thousands of people want to take the route uphill that you have. They want to reach the summit that you will be reaching very soon!

You were born to be successful. Define what you wish to achieve, cut the strings that pull you back, and set out for a journey that will change your life forever. Where you stand right now is where you need to begin!

Always remember,

"Success Begins From Where You Are!"

Conclusion

The road to success has a lot that can impede your journey uphill. There is a lot that can obstruct your path and bring you down. There are obstacles that will hold you back from beginning the journey in the first place.

But you are not going to fall back!

You are going to fight, and fight back hard. You are going to tackle what life throws at you, and flag your spot on top of Mountain Glory! And you will not stop unless you have reached what you have set out for! So grab your zest, for you will need it to reach your long-awaited destination.

To wrap it up, there is nothing in life that you cannot do or cannot become. Everything is in reach, provided you set your mind to it.

I hope that one day you will look back at this book and think of the time you began your journey, and how far you've come since then.

Good luck in all of your endeavors!

        Your friend and well-wisher,

        Michael Forde

Thank you for reading this book! If you could, please take a minute to submit a book review on www.amazon.com. It's the best way for independent authors to gain exposure. Thank you so much!

Best Wishes,

Michael Forde

Made in the USA
Middletown, DE
17 November 2017